Studies for a Self-Portrait

Rodger LeGrand

Studies for a Self-Portrait © 2019 Rodger LeGrand

Cover Design: All the Kitties

ISBN: 978-1-945917-41-7

"Making other books jealous since 2004"

Big Table Publishing Company
Boston, MA & San Francisco, CA
www.bigtablepublishing.com

Also by Rodger LeGrand

Various Ways of Thinking About the Universe
Waking Up on a Sinking Boat
Hope and Compulsion
Millions of Ravenous Creatures
Seeds
Two Thirds Water

Acknowledgments

Some of the poems in this collection originally appeared in the following literary journals: *Dash, Evening Street Review, Front Range Review, Faultline, Blue Lake Review, Scrivener Creative Review, Broad Street, Unlikely Stories,* and *Common Ground Review.*

In addition, grateful acknowledgment is made to the following publisher for printing earlier versions of some of the poems found in this collection as limited print-run chapbooks:

Two Thirds Water
Published by Flutter Press (2018)

Seeds
Published by Flutter Press (2017)

Special thanks to Frank Longo, Barbara Bergmann, Sandy Benitez, Robin Stratton, Doug Holder, Don Monaghan, Abby, Sophie, CC, Prescot, my parents—Charles and Karen LeGrand, and to Ani.

for Tom

Table of Contents

Wrinkles

Spotted mirror flecked
with toothpaste constellations
shows a face that feels borrowed.
Lines zag-a-zig it
like the muddy worm-pathed underside
of a rock, a map of caribou trails
mazing through Alaskan forests.
I tip the hourglass back to gargle
and choke my throat with sand.
Time settles where it settles—our faces,
hands, memories. Dashed lines,
second hand ticks burned into the skin
around my squinting eyes
as though I've been branded.
Is this a clock face
looking back at me?

Is that the hour hand
edging forward as I scrape
the razor along my chin
in this pre-work dance
of running out of time?

Astrophysics

He squints, but he can't tell
why the stars aligned this way.
Marriage, house, two sons and a daughter.
He squints—is that really her
seated across from him, visible but vanished
like a dead star appearing still lit centuries
after having already burned out?
Do things change that quickly? One day love,
then not? One day whole galaxies,
then empty space?
Divorced, lost house, weekends only
with the kids. But he can't tell
when it all changed and their dance
around love's event horizon—dazzled
with tingles of starshot particles,

sweet kisses, tickles—toppled into itself,
a blackhole bowing the spine back
so the heart breaks as it faces the Heavens.

Turpentine

The mirror looks finger painted,
a Van Gogh, blown ear and all,
nose from Picasso's elbow
expressionism abstracted through oils
and paperclips, a few chips
of my own reflection that bleed through
as I see me as you see me as I might be
if I were only able to get
out of my own way and down to business
and snip one of these ears already.
Lost in this streakblur mirror, stranded
on a café terrace on a starry night, arms
filled with sunflowers, leaning my head
at eternity's gate. Love colors the hideous
with magnificent possibilities.

Sedimentary Rock

Flint fragments, unwanted stones
kicked to the curb by half-flat, fat
speeding tires. What does history look like
from inside a clogged pipe? What would
the American present look like
sifted through purifying carbon filters?
The Stone Age in this age, the Flint, Michigan age.
Stone tools, cutting tools, edged blades
for removing flesh from a carcass. Smack
against steel, spark, excite, to ignite
the old factories long smothered with vines,
re-claimed by trees. To breathe
sooty exhaust again, to hear the shift-ending
whistle again. Time doesn't tick backward,
sediment doesn't roll uphill.

The media might have stopped
covering it, but if I were you,
I still wouldn't drink that water.

That Night at The Malt House in Yonkers

First glance ignites. Slow-
ly. Sharply. How fire burns.
Fuel. In a wildfire
fallen trees, dried leaves.
For us, line of sight—eye
contact, body and body.
Miles plays over the banter
of the after-work crowd.
I see you at the bar
grabbing our pint glasses
and for a moment
don't realize it's you
I'm seeing. Burning
by the molecule, oxygen
combusting in a fury of sparks

turning to flames. So taken by you
that to see you across the bar this way
is to see you for the first time.
Heat. Convection through liquid,
the clink of glasses.
Waves of heat radiate, rotate
out as though vibrations from the sunset
spiraling past Venus's densely
packed atmosphere.
Conduction. Heat transfer
between two objects,
two bodies, in direct
physical contact.
You come back to our table,
smiling at me smiling at you.

Tidal Angels

Lava forms incomprehensible islands
at the corners of her eyelids.
A salt-streaked archipelago of tears.
Waves, the moon's wings,
unroll at her feet, then up
the slope of her shins, onion bulb thighs.
She keeps walking, up to her chin
and further, submerged in the dark water
that feels against her skin
like raindrops falling into themselves
as the moon thumps wave after wave,
its heavy wings beating.

New England Winter

House creaks. Draft
blows through
like it owns the place.
The snow feels lighter,
the wind somehow warmer
the more I make the weather
my own. Align with it
and there's no cold
beyond me to shiver against.
The mouse in the kitchen
feels differently. Last night
it scratched its initials
into the breadbox.

Halo Feathers

Line between over preening
and self-mutilation
measured in plucks.
Birdy body without feathers
gets thinner and thinner.
Pink belly flesh, dimples
where feathers once grew,
flightless in an iron prison.
Caged birds do this sometimes,
the madness of *Polly wanna a cracker*
when all Polly really wanna do
is soar above a thick canopy of trees.
Only its head remains untouched,
small pristine feathers, halo feathers,
an unpreened crown for a queen
with no subjects. Everywhere I go

I can imagine the outlines of angels,
watching over us, silent as shadows.
In the hopelessness of their cause,
do they, too, reach back and pluck feathers
from once stunning wings?

Moon Glow Ocean

Transformation.
Her palms just above
my shoulder blades
become wings for my anxiety
to take flight. We fly this way,
embered evening, blaze
of tree-lined coastal
haze slowly burning out,
waves roll, lava forms new islands.
Her palms, wings
turning to rose petals
that cradle my fall into the calm,
moon glow ocean.
Every star, four of Jupiter's moons,
sing to us as we drift in our rose petal lifeboat.
Counting stars, counting spirals

of planets, sea shells
sparkling in the vastness,
ancient mollusks
suspended in the black canopy
that drapes over us like her eyelids,
lashes brushing my arm.

The Shape of a Poem

Some poems start out zoomed in
on a small detail, the ridged knob
off the end of a radiator, calcified
underneath from years of a persistent,
indecipherable leak, and then the poem
might move outward to the thumping
drip of a faucet, then to Niagara River
rushing toward an eternally split horizon,
its horseshoe edge, then to oceans
churning miles below Europa's
iced surface, or water trapped, frozen,
on a flung-wide comet. It's in
the details where we find ourselves,
in the vastness we hope to get lost.

Sea Without Water

Imagine wrinkles
without time
or dying
without having lived.
Imagine the sea
without water, wings
without bird. Rain
without clouds,
bruise without touch.

Coasting the Blind Spot

How long have you drifted there,
behind me and to the left, oblivious,
lost in front of a dashboard of screaming fans?
When I check the mirrors, first the back
then the side, a quick peek over my shoulder,
I begin lopsiding left. You swerve
and for the first time I see your car,
see your face, frozen, a vowel
projected from the diaphragm
sustained above your dashboard.
We correct ourselves, return to our lanes.
For a moment I can see you in the mirror,
the band warming back up
as you drum the steering wheel,
your front seat stadium
chanting your name.

Then you vanish again,
a freeway ghost song
coasting the blind spot.

Seeds

Wakefulness rises
the way a maple tree grows.
Rehearsed since the first tree
emerged, a process of seeds
descending to the ground
the way leaves fall.
Maple tree helicopters,
singular rotation, spirals,
soft landing in grass
and dried leaves
where some will reach out
of themselves, vibrant, almost
glowing green, the start
of a vine, the first root, thick
like a new back tooth,
that will seek water, soil, light,

press into the earth, find
the true meaning of itself
in dirt. Sky and earth. Sun
and moon. First leaf will form
by two inches. Years will pass.
This tree will grow, change, find
and lose its shape. New branches
will sprout off into more new branches—
decades of leaves falling, and its insides
marking itself with rings
for each year, each layer
of growth. This is how time passes.
In the beginning seeds fall
and anything's possible.
Eventually it's our leaves that fall.

DIY

Takes the chisel
and mallet, kneels
in his overalls,
blade angled
to get the right line.
His future, an oval
slab of granite.
Swings
the mallet,
initials
chipped in.
Hard work,
but some things
are better done yourself.

Alone for the Commute

Empty train and this guy
decides to sit next to me
without seeming to notice
he has his pick. Could stretch-
out on a three-seater,
could take in the sights,
snowy egret that curves
above Walker Pond
or lily pads encased
in thin, glass frost.
Maybe he knows something I don't?
Maybe this will help first responders
find the bodies if our train
goes off the rails, the two of us
sidebyshoulder for our final trip to work?
I angle at him, about to tell him

to move, but I can see it in his eyes
as he stares straight ahead.
Sometimes people have a hard time
being alone. So, we sit like this,
neither of us talking,
both pretending
we're the only ones here.

The Pivot

The air, easier to breathe.
On the side of my neck
your stars, small kisses.
Lost in the found expansiveness of you.
Your stars, small kisses
on the side of my neck
and the air, easier to breathe,
back when you loved me.

Pick Quick

In the hot, cramped bathroom
of a poorly lit trailer, mid-august
when every day seemed to last years,
we wrapped ourselves in heavy wool blankets
and spun in circles, chanting:
Bloody Mary, Bloody Mary, Bloody Mary.
The Legend: after a three count, stop
see the disfigured, blood and pock-marked,
washed-out face of a woman, Bloody
Mary, as she was known
by the kids in my neighborhood,
the kidnapper, the eater of children's souls.
My imagination what it was—vivid,
tactile—I could see her in the mirror
with each spin, could see her behind my eyelids
when I kept them shut. When we finished

our spins and chants, we screamed at our own
terrified reflections. And we heard
the screams of other children
from beyond the mirror, beyond
the thin trailer walls.
Had the mirror become a bridge
to the unknown? We spun again
and again, chanting with the urgency:
Bloody Mary, Bloody Mary, Bloody Mary!
Free them! A shadow formed
on the bathroom's closed blinds.
Peeking out into the glare of the noon sun
we saw the kids next door getting slapped
for feeding their dog too early. No
hidden dimension. No pock-marked
bloody face replacing our reflection
in the cracked mirror. Only us
and the trailer park—our universe.
So we scraped together as many pennies
as we could find and ran
to the corner store,

Pick Quick, to buy
watermelon jaw breakers
for five cents.

Aging

Each snowflake, its own shape,
distinguishable from all others,
until it lands on the bank
of the Merrimack river,
folds into other snowflakes
that also landed, having lulled
through branches to settle
where they would settle.
As soon as they form they begin
to lose themselves.
We sit on the banks of our own rivers
and wrap our memories silent,
each, too, with their own shape,
inside fallen leaves and float them across
the soon to be frozen water.

Pores

Last night I woke at some painted, dark hour.
It felt like my soul had poured out
through the pores at the top of my head,
so I looked under the bed,
checked behind the shower curtain
and the closet door where the linens
pile into wrinkles. No luck. So I shuck
the pores from my corncob arms and legs
with a potato peeler, let them fall into a bucket,
these smallest entries of me, smallest exits.
If I roll them together, a doughy ball
of openings, could I make a larger portal
to pull my wandering soul back into me?
What would that other side of me
look like? Would I find my soul there,
seated at a small wooden table

eating soup after she died,
an elbow of torn bread off to the side,
or would something else be there waiting,
a hungry look in its shredded smile,
alone, watching me, alone, watch it?

Memory's Abandoned Building

That's what happens when people
forget things. Weeds, vines reclaim
an abandoned building.
Tree roots push through floorboards.
The shape of the structure vaguely there,
but unrecognizable. To see it—
rotten support beams moss-lined, rain
cutting through empty air
that the roof once covered—
is to fill in the blanks. Maybe
imagine light falling through the windows
on a warm spring day, dust motes
suspended in the glare. Maybe
picture the floor boards, solid oak
under your feet. Or a family,
kids playing in a bedroom, parents

together, slicing vegetables
in the kitchen, the smell of peppers,
onions, ginger. Fill in the architecture
with what suits you, fill in the moments
spent living, spent together, because
that's all we have left—the imagining.
Once forgotten, all we can do is imagine a story
and tell it to the horned owl
perched overhead on a last,
rotting beam, though even the owl
will look down at you, doubting the details.

In Line Waiting for Salvation

Chest to back for eternity.
An endless line
on an endless subway platform
waiting for Godot or to go next?
Shuffle-foot forward
every millennium
or so. Lines. Our straight line
across a curved world,
into a vacuum state of energy
spiked through the largest atom,
the universe, or the smallest? Lines.
A line of geese clunking across the morning.
Curved red line where her favorite dress
meets her thigh. Vein line beneath
wax paper skin. 29 Powder blue horizons
falling down the page. A line of thought, line

of sight. One line breaks,
blends into white space
and dangles for a breath.
Then another?
Is that the answer? Continue putting
everything in line? One line,
then the next. Highway lines
painted over and painted again.
Soup kitchen lines, ladled up and marching
into battle. A line of thread
from a shirt sleeve. The line from Freeport, IL
to Jupiter's eternal tornado.
A line of poetry, a line of cold mud
shaken off a boot. Silence
between two people
after a lifetime together,
the way a fault line opens
and fills with rain.

Ocean Love Story

Your right arm entwined
in my left or my arms
entwined in the might be
dockside morning sun
sat in mutual lotus, wrapped
in each the other.
Tangled seaweed limbs
drip into the deep.
Shark season.
We wait for a great white
to bite the lips off our toes,
which kiss blindly
in the unimaginable darkness
just beneath the water's surface.

Tongue

A weird word to spell.
The mouth muscle,
to lick, taste, speak.
Today I tongue the empty
spaces where my teeth
used to be, a graveyard
with missing tombstones.
Near death from a cracked tooth,
blood tooth, infected
tooth. In recovery,
the feeling of your laugh
bounces through my chest
and I want it to stay there,
to line the inside of my body.

I'll ask Eric Guntor
if he can tattoo your laugh
onto my left ventricle.

Philadelphia Haiku

The smell of rain against hot asphalt.
First night pulling tricks—
tomorrow the kids will have breakfast.

Graveyard for Mundane Memories

Where days go to die, where I
place my oversized
canned ham head
to suffocate the daylight
and the havoc it photosynthesized—
commuter rail grime,
greasy slice of cheesie for lunch,
all of it, choked out
beneath the weight
of my heavy, ground beef skull.
Next morning, it's night's turn.
I murder it when I make my bed,
take its breath the way flood waters
take coastal cities. Fluffed pillows,
tombstones. Then the corkscrew turns.
New day. Coffee. Shower. Commuter rail.

Just wait, I say under my breath,
eager for my next kill, to hear the day
gasp and claw for air when I curl up,
bury my graveyard of mundane memories
in feathers. Unless I die today,
I'll murder this one and tomorrow, too,
and if I'm lucky, the one after that,
and if I'm lucky....

Message in a Bottle

To fill every page, millions
of loose leaves, all the same,
scribbled over and over
like tide rolling in or out,
the moon's influence
driving the oceans mad with indecision.
How could you, on each note in longhand,
stuffed into corked, glass bottles
and tossed into the Sea of Tranquility.
Millions of bottles. Millions of words
all the same, stinging silent
in the moon's empty atmosphere,
in an empty sea, no life, no chance
of a response, millions of notes,

screaming to be read, stinging
in unison, *How could you? How could you?*
Except one. *I miss you.*

Falling

What if this perfect fall day,
pumpkin and apricot
colored trees, a few
deep red like apples,
never began
and would never end?
Always 10:02 AM
in this museum of us,
an exhibit label
stuck to the wall by co-curators:
I Love You, I Love You, I Love You.

Entanglement

The surf foamed as it rushed
toward the wide, jagged rocks
just below the window by our table.
I hadn't noticed the waitress
standing over me while I was lost
in the movement of water
breathing in from the depths
while you were off to wash your hands
before dinner. High tide here
means low tide somewhere else.
One big ocean-sized pot tipping
side to side. Which made me think about
quantum entanglement. Entangled
particles are always connected.
If something happens to this side of the ocean,
something also happens to the other side.

The water line in Portland entangled
with the coastal rocks along distant continents.
You were off running your hands under water,
I was at the table, submerged
in my watery thoughts.
When you returned we ordered.
Drank wine. Ate shellfish
and pasta. Even separated by great distances
two entangled particles
will affect each the other.
How the thought of you emerges
if I'm having a bad moment in a bad day.
How if you smile, I smile, if sadness
enwraps you like kelp, then I, too, drown within it.
How seeing you cross the restaurant
to return to your seat magnetically
pulls my heart to beat faster.

I Don't Want to Be a Fat Corpse

A rectangle of earth
pulled from the ground
like a tooth. Grass scent of summer
making its turn toward cooler months,
leaves quilting a blanket for the ego
to fall upon. Who will remember you?
Great grandparents' wedding photo
hanging on the wall, early 1900's, all these years
and now with no children, I'll be the last
to see this photo. There's no one next in line
to search for meaning in it, to look for a hint
of resemblance. Handmade wedding dress, bouquet
of hand-picked flowers. Everything was by hand
back then. Black and white, matte print.
No smiles. Still, expressionless.
I don't want to be a fat corpse,

which I can clearly imagine
given the circumference
of my waistline. Energy never ends.
It transforms. Me and my excess padding
converted into fuel. Me into mucus
and rotting flesh. Me into an oblivion
of shallow breathing, of chocolate pudding memories.
The couple in the photo, though, pinned beneath
a glass frame, younger then than I am now,
and lean, on the verge of starvation
but somehow they survived, until
this broken branch of their family tree.
The finality of me: Here I am. Heavier
than both of them combined.
Their success, their survival, embodied
in my waistline and in me also
they would find their demise.
No children. I am where
the family lineage ends.
My only grace—imagining
transformation. I'll be a metamorphosis,

a moonlit moth flinging itself back
into its cocoon, an accumulation
of rationalities, of should haves, of
laziness, the terror of confronting
the nothingness that sits soundless
on a blank page. *Fat corpse, fat corpse.*
Stone cut into a slanted, half oval
with a few words chiseled
below my birth and death dates:
Who will tend your weeds? Who will burn
incense in your memory? Who will set flowers
at your head? No, no. Only the worms
will visit. I only have faith in you,
Mr. Worm, Simic wrote.
They'll come for a while
until even they have no reason
to stay. I read a letter from the man in the photo
to his bride: "…the sun setting over your shoulder
in the mirror. I can remember every time
I saw your face from this particular angle.
If I could leave anything to you

to hold onto and remember of me,
it would be how I feel
when I see you this way."

Digging a River

Never standstillness
of a rock-wombed spring,
sprung along the mountain's edge.
A cut artery. From mountain to sea,
rivers always change. I want my life
to be a river, carved out naturally
from a glacier's century-long glide
across a shifting continent.
How many glaciers remain,
how many centuries? If I'm lucky,
I have a few decades at best.
So, I push my cupped hands
through the grass,
into hard-packed dirt
and dig.

Raindrop Clocks

Yesterday the wind mini-tornadoed
every leaf that had fallen
from memory's tree.
I tried to rake them,
but each time I got a decent pile together
the wind would do its dance,
a waltz, a twirl,
beat time on my head
like Roethke's poem.
So I went to the doctor
for a prescription to treat wasted time
since there isn't much left
to waste. Damp leaves
across the front yard.

Each raindrop its own clock.
Each leaf a piece of me
one day I'll forget.

Urinal Cake Salesman

Another of history's potentially great
accordion players lost
to paycheck-to-paycheck living.
Instead, this is his life's work.
"Little bundt cake, little bundt cake,"
he swoons as he swaddles the
minty cocoon into its porcelain cradle.
Hospitals. Schools. Malls. Stadiums.
We fabricate fantasies of our worth
when our unimportance gives us the flush.
What he does with these cakes,
he does for humanity's sake
while the accordion plagues the back of his mind
with music he'll never write. Instead,
his contribution to the world, he tells himself,

because he needs to tell himself something,
refresh our lives, little bundt cake,
one urinal at a time.

Jenna's Story

Hearing her story,
I could picture the details: her arms
didn't flap. She kept them wrapped
tightly around her teddy bear.
Only a few seconds,
but *only* lasted long enough
that she felt the weightlessness
pull her heart up
behind her ears
while she looked back
at the sun's glare off the brick
apartment building,
at her brothers' thin, dry faces
hanging from the second-floor window
like potted plants
needing to be watered.

Within seconds her skull
smack-bounced
off the sidewalk on 52nd and Walnut.
Who knows why
her brothers thought it would be fun
to push their little sister out the window?
And now, almost two decades later,
she lives downstairs from us,
an adult surviving on public assistance
in a brain trauma rehab program
so she can learn to take care of herself.
I've seen the paper work,
since she leaves her open mail
in the stairwell we share.
Men come by and grunt, groan, grunt
every day, every night. Some
pay—we can hear them
counting their ones through our open window.
Some just leave. Tonight, she tells us this story
while she sits drunk on our apartment floor.
She was crying in the stairwell

and said she'd lost her keys.
Ani invited her in, to keep her safe,
because that's how she is with people in need.
I would have left her outside
to fend for herself. She sprawls
on the floor mumbling her way into blackout
and knocks her handbag over, apartment keys
rattling their way to the carpet.

Spilled Moon

Lights out and moonlight spills
through the blinds like milk,
a ladder of white-blue light
across the hardwood floor.
Where might it lead
if I were to climb
past the windowsill?
A soft-sand bed at the edge
of the Sea of Tranquility?
To the moon's dark side?
To tomorrow and the morning sun
that will rise, as it does, the same way
every morning? Or to a few years ago
when we were happy and excited
just to know the other existed?
One person always loves the other more.

You're in the next room
talking to someone on the phone.
I hear you say my name so softly
that it feels like I don't actually exist.

Salt Deposits

Thin cuts of lace hang from the clouds
by cobweb string. Snowflakes
in slow motion. We catch them,
unravel each intricate
impossibility with the warmth
of our clasped hands.
Crude, oil slick tongues
paint our chins black
as we pant. The price of our
everything renaissance,
our nail scratches on the wall
in history's backroom as we claw
our way up and out of poverty,
disease, our human/animal need
to feed our bellies with more.
There's always a price,

and someone always comes to collect.
The rest of our breathable days
we'll shovel salt with our eyelashes.

Long in the Dirt

An archeologist digs
the ruins of a Viking village,
shovels at first and then
small handheld brooms
for dusting around fragile finds—
bead trinkets, ladle, petrified
leather shoe. The owners,
long in the dirt themselves,
likely imagined they would be remembered,
that the beaded bracelet
handed down to little Helga
would have then been handed down
to Helga's child and then
to that child's child,
generations linked by touch
without ever actually touching.

We might find their remains,
but they aren't remembered,
covered with mounds of dirt
with the inevitable laying to rest
a life of daily living, worries,
ancient love, exhaustion,
as will also be true for each of us,
so that we too are linked
without ever actually touching.

Folie à Deux

Twittered together in sickness
and in wealth. Sea salt sanctions,
sea green clouds exploding
over red rocks while a waltz
plays a onetwothree onetwothree
across the landscape—dune
primrose viola, rock daisy
violin. One two tweet. One
two tweet. Repurposed
in this landscape,
large-headed Oedipal twins.
Either might accomplish
what neither of their fathers
could. Crack of thunder
two three. Acid rain,
two three, two, one....

Staying or Leaving

The color of the soles of her feet
came out of the sky
on one of those evenings
when everyone knows
tomorrow it will rain.

Sentencing

The sentence is in custody
of an idea, celled in,
a capital letter slammed shut
by a period. The semi-colon slices
the idea's wrist, spills its meaning,
bleeds between bars
in this system of meaningless meanings,
laws, paragraphs of mandatory
minimum sentences.
Private prisons make private profits
detaining private citizens.
Thousands of souls
in custody of prison sentences.
None in custody of themselves.
Profit. A one-word sentence.

This is what the American Dream
has become, writing prison sentences
into the stock exchange.

Darkness

I had a dream, which was not at all a dream.
The bright sun was extinguished, and the stars
Did wander darkling in the eternal space....
—George Gordon, Lord Byron

Heart monitor beeps a steady click
and I can no longer here it.
I leap inward and impale myself on the pointed
pickaxe of my brainstem. A broken tooth
became infected. The infection
entered my blood. At first, pain
is part of me the way my hands are part of me,
of my body, as I flail wildly toward
an unknowing transcendence of otherworldly
numbness. I am numb to myself, my life,
my body, my counterfeit ruminations,
and I transcend my heart, my teeth, my
broken teeth, my bacterial blood.

The pain radiates inward, somehow outward
simultaneously, a paradox of direction
and intention, so that it renders itself
nothingness. I am nothing. In this swirl
I'm settled beyond my control. Acceptance:
how small is my life? Only a handful of people
will notice the absence I'll leave.
Blackness unfolds like origami wings
that reach from the base of my skull
and around, up slowly around
my head, blinding my periphery.
Framed, pathless, in tepid darkness, my tub
filling with starless exuberance. I can only see
in front of me and visibility is low.
Sinking. Numbness. Quicksand
numbness. It feels like dozing after a long,
39-year day. And it's warming, lightless warmth
of dust cooking. Imagine a furnace igniting
into the cold start of winter after months
of dormancy. Body on automatic.
Brain cannibalized. The paradox

of this vacancy—I am freed
from myself, from my cranked-up brain,
from worry about bills and paychecks,
about even this sinking pit of me
lined with unread poems, this abyss
of moonless, eternal space, the sound of nurses
preparing me, my body, this other thing,
for surgery. No beacon of light to guide
my journey. No angels or demons
to point the right direction.
Only warm, soft sleep that goes so deep
dreams can't reach, that I can't reach,
filled with waves of stagnant air, handfuls
of dark, endless clouds rolling over dark,
endless clouds, rolling over dark
endless clouds, rolling over me.

Basic Math

You $=$ need to control.
Mow the lawn,
conquer nature.
Arithmetic of your force
in this world, a sugar-filled ass
imposed on nature $=$ mass times
velocity of this whoopie pie
(or insert sweet tasty
yum yum of choice)
$\div$ by the square root of
the ∞ voice in the back
of your ∞ head, a voice$^{\infty}$
that every second bigbangexplodes
a new universe of intrusion across
your mental landscape. Mow
the lawn. Control the earth

and when finished
kick back with a beer-ski
and look up to name the stars,
control the aeronautics
of the blackened night sky,
infinite clusters of expanding,
contracting, extracting
galaxies. Control the cosmic hum
of the universe's vibration, its wiggle,
vibrating at a frequency
that might sound
like a humming bird's buzzed
nectar quest, a brook
flooding in early spring.
Mow the lawn while that voice
chisels as at it chatters.
It knows gravity is gravity
without you. Rivers
accumulate flood waters
without you. The sun burns
and illuminates the solar system

without you. And the universe − (minus,
minus, minus) you
still = the universe.

Marcus Pamiglio's Left Foot

with its truck bed toenails,
bullied his right. Marcus the turkey foot,
Marcus with arms for toes.
The doctors had thought Marcus' left foot
was a twin sister who died in the womb,
just a mound of flesh in a belly.
Marcus the Frankenfoot, Marcus
the lunchbox foot. As an infant,
his parents, with normal feet, kept him covered
in layers of blankets. By the time
he entered elementary school,
Marcus knew his foot,
knew he wouldn't play
with the other kids, knew how expensive
his shoes were. Marcus
the drawbridge foot. Marcus the sidewalk foot.

Marcus: the foot that dragged behind, too heavy
for his small leg to lift, bumbling
on the playground, tossing leaves
over his head, trying to catch them
between his lips.

Minutiae

A solitary moth
circles, circles
before vanishing
into the candle's
flame. In an ocean
of galaxies two
white-hot stars collide.
Nothing so small
it lacks meaning
and nothing so large
as not to appear humbled
next to the enormity
of the cosmos. It's context.
Minutiae—the quick extinction
of a moth's seemingly irrelevant life.
Minutiae—two stars melt

into each the other, shared gravity,
ripping them into a void
where light is no longer possible.
Who are we to expect more?

You Didn't Tell Me

I don't know how to write this poem,
if that's what this is. Would it be better
as a letter? Where would I send it?
You're dead now.
If you were alive
would you prefer this
as letter, poem, carved
into a Grecian urn, or blown glass
filled with a final exhale?
Here's the thing.
I didn't know you were dying.
You left that out of your final letter,
which was sweet and generous, as always,
but you left it out like some casual detail
not worth the effort, like not troubling to mention
the line at the grocery store was longer

than you had expected. Keats
was swallowed whole by his lungs, too.
I wonder if he kept it secret?
It's been years and I still catch myself
waiting to hear your booming voice
tell me this wasn't the end of a great poem
that I'll never again read.
I would have ripped my lungs out
for you to have one more breath.

Baby Elephant

Trunk too short for its baby body,
grabbing hold of its mother's tail
while it looks around, the way
littles ones do. A chain,
too tight, shackled
to Baby Elephant's leg.
The chain hurts to pull against.
Wounds open. Baby Elephant
stops fighting. Years later,
full grown, the original chain,
tiny now compared to the elephant's
massive bulk, still wraps once
around the leg.
Memory of that earlier pain,
the failure, the sense
of being trapped, broken

inside, keeps Baby Elephant
from breaking free.
Chained to memories.
This is how we live.

Tricuspid Blues

Audience, silent at tonight's
performance. The surgeon
fingers the valves, a trumpet
without a rhythm section.
Massages with her bare hands
the heart, caresses
with gentle purpose
a rhythmic shuffle beat
to syncopate this muted muscle.
The greats run scales through her inner ear—
Miles, Coltrane. Her operating jazz band,
though, hums John Cage's
Four Minutes, Thirty-Three Seconds
with closed eyes, slapping open palms

on skinless, soundless drums,
never to thump a tempo,
never again to tango.

Apoptosis

Programmed to absorb
our own dead cells.
I am the compilation of dead cells
from my meager beginnings
absorbed into a plump, gill-less body.
Adulted life. Squished into roles I might play
to fit the way I'm expected to fit,
limits pressed into time
like a diecast stamp. I can't.
The pointy spines on my imagined cathedral
won't allow it no matter how hard you insist.
Looking at you is how burnt chicken
feels against my tongue.
Synesthesia of sight and taste.
Charred, flightless bird, fleshed,
a mess of ravaged tissue. I need

to metamorph my me memories
so me can be fitted with the right look
for the right part and put the right words
in the right order. Kafka had his roach.
Took gold in the metaphorm Olympics.
All the academics argue whose self
best imposes on that metaphor
to metaphorm the roachiest.
You think of me as a tadpole,
pollywogging my way
across a mud puddle, waiting
on my slick, fat froggy belly
for your advice to fiberglass
a proper aquarium around me.
Become a frog? Franz Frogka?
I am not the tadpole to your roach.
I am the dead cells absorbed into me,
that define me, the dead cells
of the last ten dead years
and counting. Apoptosis:
my body, soul, rancid

slick belly. I've come this far
and don't need your advice.
Poetry didn't die with Pound.
Leave me to read.
Leave me for dead.

Linekin Bay, Maine

—with Henry

Trees along the shoreline,
luminous, molten,
early morning blown-glass reflections
on the water's surface.
No wind, no people.
Greeted by a lone porpoise
that hardly makes a ripple
as its dorsal fin feels for sunlight.
Boaters have left for the season.
Lobster traps have been slugged
from the water. The season changes
as it always does, the way the sun rises
as it always does. A few half-sleeping
cormorants slap their wings

against the water's surface,
a sounding drum keeping time.
Winter will be here soon.

Fallen Cubes

A few leaves turned early
this year, starbursts
of gold, red, honey
blended with muted green
in the end-of-summer
canopy above us.
Squares on the calendar loosen like teeth.
Fallen cubes stacked in a wobbly tower
like a child had been playing
with blocks. The cold
will topple the days, bury us
in ice, wind. Fire crackles. Knit
blankets. We'll settle into ourselves,
knowing more cubes have fallen
than remain stacked on unturned pages.

Massachusetts

Longing for the bitter cold,
evergreens damp with snow,
a morning fire
burning seasoned wood.
Beyond the frost-lined
windowpanes, pines
and spruce stand dark, towering
next to bare maples that retreat
into themselves for quarter
of the year. Living without seasons
is being cemented in time—no sense
of the earth revolving.
Seasonal change, a cosmic wristwatch
ticking the seconds.
In New England

you can feel time passing,
can see, smell, taste it
on the chilled morning air.

At Opposition

Roof deck of our apartment building
overlooking the Benjamin Franklin Bridge.
Camden across the Delaware River. Reality,
the fuzzy growl as train cars
rock down the bridge's slope.
We found each other again.
Mars and Saturn burn
through our binoculars,
and I imagine Stanley Kunitz
standing on his roof as a child,
waiting for Halley's Comet,
waiting the world to end.
We stand beneath
a fat red globe tied
to an invisible string,
high above Philadelphia's

1,526,006 people. Mars,
opposite the sun, at its closest point
to the Earth, at opposition,
at its closest point to us standing silent
in contrast to the caustic blasts
of stalled traffic on the Ben Franklin,
in contrast to the orange
and white helicopters chopping the air
as they patrol the Delaware, us in contrast
to the other worldly state of politics
and how people treat each other,
in contrast to work and bills, positioned
this way between another world
and this world, so many drifting,
distant vacuous bodies
at opposition to each other and themselves,
to us, alone on this rooftop deck,
waiting for the world to end.

The Last Day of the Great Poet,
Mr. Weldon Kees

Four seconds of breathless gravity
before your body vanished
into the Pacific.
Four seconds—a line of poetry,
a few notes splashed
on the piano, turquois or orange
dotting canvas. You felt the way
we all sometimes feel,
the way I'm feeling right now.
I read your poems to quiet my mind.
Sometimes I can picture the sound
and feel the wind in your face,
as though it's my face, me falling,
my four seconds of gravity, water
getting closer, a last line of poetry

printing on the back of my eyelids,
like so many others,
never making it to the page.

New Pens

Good morning,
blank page.
I greet you
with a rainy smile,
with scribbles
in blue ink,
then black.
I plan to test
a pack of new pens,
leaving you bruised
and battered
with each
tattered word.

Sleepwalking

At some point last night
in a dream or awake
or hovering
somewhere in between
I began to roam
the apartment.
Sleepwalking?
I think I might have
dusted a little,
maybe run the vacuum.
And I cleaned out
the refrigerator,
needed to make room
for a sack of dreams
to store in the crisper
to keep them fresh

as long as possible,
since I no longer have the energy
to pretend they might become real.
After all this time
when I wake up
I can still feel your body
next to mine.

Old Books

I flung myself
into boxes of old books
today. Volumes of poems racked
in torn cardboard boxes squealed
with packing tape.
Old friends had come for a visit,
so it was only polite to put on tea.
So many now dead or still dead, and most
I only knew through printed words
on dusty pages. We'd met years ago
at old bookstores in the Village
or Philadelphia or Boston.
I learned from you
how to feel about words,
how to let words help me
to feel about the world.

Some of my favorite memories
were finding you hiding in dark,
empty bookstores. I can smell
the stale, musty air, while I sit on my sofa,
chamomile tea steeping.
Who I am now comes from having met you,
line by syllable by line by breath.
To stumble upon you this way
feels like my chest has been cracked open
like the torn cardboard boxes
in which you now reside.
A sea of memories washes through me
like I'm not even here. I'll return you
to the darkness of these boxes
now that the tea's gone cold.
We all have our graves.

About the Author

Rodger LeGrand studied writing at Sarah Lawrence College and the State University of New York at Oswego. He has taught at MIT, the University of Pennsylvania, the University of the Arts, Temple University, and North Carolina State University. You can reach him at www.RodgerLeGrand.com.

Made in the USA
Lexington, KY
20 November 2019